Global connections

Teens in

Argentina

by Danielle Smith-Llera

Content Adviser: David William Foster,
Professor of Spanish and Women and
Gender Studies, Arizona State University

Reading Adviser: Alexa L. Sandmann, Ed.D.,
Professor of Literacy, College and Graduate
School of Education, Health, and Human Services,
Kent State University

Compass Point Books ✦ Minneapolis, Minnesota

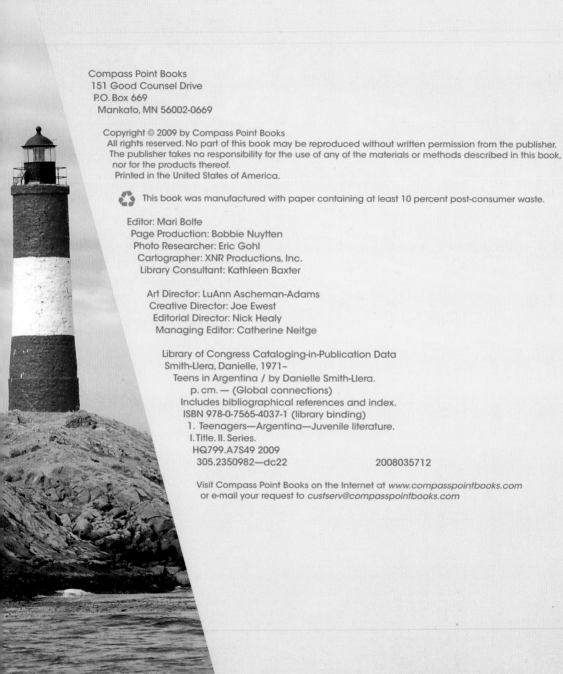

Compass Point Books
151 Good Counsel Drive
P.O. Box 669
Mankato, MN 56002-0669

This book was manufactured with paper containing at least 10 percent post-consumer waste.

Editor: Mari Bolte
Page Production: Bobbie Nuytten
Photo Researcher: Eric Gohl
Cartographer: XNR Productions, Inc.
Library Consultant: Kathleen Baxter

Art Director: LuAnn Ascheman-Adams
Creative Director: Joe Ewest
Editorial Director: Nick Healy
Managing Editor: Catherine Neitge

Library of Congress Cataloging-in-Publication Data
Smith-Llera, Danielle, 1971–
    Teens in Argentina / by Danielle Smith-Llera.
        p. cm. — (Global connections)
    Includes bibliographical references and index.
    ISBN 978-0-7565-4037-1 (library binding)
        1. Teenagers—Argentina—Juvenile literature.
    I. Title. II. Series.
    HQ799.A7S49 2009
        305.2350982—dc22   2008035712

Visit Compass Point Books on the Internet at *www.compasspointbooks.com*
or e-mail your request to *custserv@compasspointbooks.com*

Table of Contents

PACIFIC
OCEAN

PERU

BOLIVIA

PARAGUAY

CHIL

URUG

ARGENTINA

★ Buenos Aires

FALKLAND ISLAND

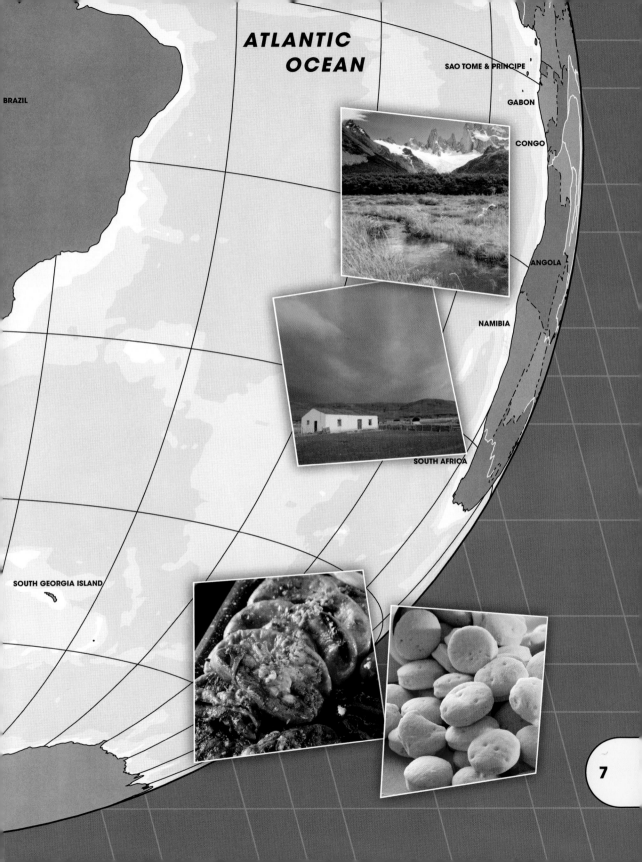

ATLANTIC
OCEAN

SAO TOME & PRINCIPE

BRAZIL

GABON

CONGO

ANGOLA

NAMIBIA

SOUTH AFRICA

SOUTH GEORGIA ISLAND

ARGENTINA'S MILLIONS OF CATTLE, FERTILE FIELDS, AND PETROLEUM RESERVES MAKE IT ONE OF LATIN AMERICA'S WEALTHIEST COUNTRIES. Argentina also puts great effort into tapping another rich resource: its young people. Almost a quarter of the country's nearly 40.7 million people are under age 14. Argentina is committed to their education, boasting one of the world's highest literacy rates. More than 97 percent of Argentines age 15 and older can read. This multicultural country offers its teens a rich heritage.

The vast majority of Argentina's teens live in cities, either in gated estates or slums. Rural teens may live on sprawling farms or in dirt-floor huts. Despite a strong economy, many struggle to finish school and find jobs. Regardless, Argentine families prize their children. They know that the young hold the country's future as it struggles to realize its potential.

9

Nearly 10 million students attend school in Argentina.

1

School for All

guardapolvos
(gwahr-thah-POL-bos)

YOUNG PEOPLE ARRIVE AT SCHOOL FROM ALL OVER THE SPRAWLING ARGENTINE CAPITAL OF BUENOS AIRES. They travel by foot, bus, subway, or a parent's car. Students are easy to spot. Public school students wear short white jackets called *guardapolvos* to keep their clothes clean. The front pockets are crammed with snacks and school supplies. With these uniforms, the Argentine government shows it treats all students the same, regardless of their background. Public education is free and required for ages 5 to 14.

Nearly all children in Argentina complete the seven years of elementary school. The government's dedication to quality public education dates back nearly 150 years. Today's youth take education seriously, as do their parents, who are usually well educated.

Though most of Argentina's children learn to read, 20 percent of teens do not attend secondary school. Some cannot afford school supplies and must work

There are public and private schools for both primary- and secondary- level students.

instead. Others in remote areas find it difficult to get to school, but the government continues to make efforts to educate its teens.

The school year runs from March to December, which in the Southern Hemisphere is fall to early summer. Students spend most of each day in the same classroom. Teachers come to them, rotating between rooms, with a three-minute break between lessons.

Students attend school in shifts—as many as three students may use the same desk during the day. The first shift attends school from 8 A.M. to noon, then returns home. The afternoon shift arrives at 1 P.M. and stays until 5 P.M. Some schools offer an evening shift as well.

Students in Argentina's secondary schools study the same general subjects

Teen Scenes

A 15-year-old girl wakes in her bedroom in a spacious brick house in a northern suburb of Buenos Aires. A wide, green yard can be seen out the window. Although her closet is full of clothing from the nearby shopping mall, which carries the latest European fashions, she pulls on the uniform for her private school. She then bolts down the coffee and toast set out by a maid.

After breakfast, she and her father head downtown in an air-conditioned electric train. The girl gets off at the stop for her school, waving goodbye to her father. She knows that in a city full of highly educated people, finding rewarding work can be a challenge. Although many of her friends dream of becoming models, she takes her science classes seriously. She hopes to one day join the growing number of female doctors.

One bus stop away, a 15-year-old boy wakes in a room he shares with three siblings. The house's walls are made of sheet metal from old advertising signs. There is no light to turn on. There is no running water for washing. His father is lucky to have work, though as a low-paid construction worker. He walks out onto the unpaved streets before the afternoon shift at his public school. He hopes to earn a few pesos washing cars. This money helps buy his school uniform and books.

Both of these teens lived through the economic crisis of 2001, when more than half the country was driven into poverty. The crisis affected them in different ways, however. As teens living in today's Argentina, they know education is crucial if they are to find work and help their country's economic stability.

Timetable of a School Day

Students with an afternoon school shift begin school in the afternoon, rather than in the morning.

6:30 A.M.	Rise and have a light breakfast, if any
8 A.M.	Attend four-hour school day
12 P.M.	Play after-school sports or meet up with friends at a sports club
1 P.M.	Have lunch at home and a period of rest; work on homework
5 P.M.	Snack at home; chat with friends on the Internet or meet up with classmates to work on school projects
9 P.M.	Have a multiple-course dinner at home with family

at either a "basic" or "higher" level. The Argentine National Council of Education sets the curriculum for both public and private schools. In the last two years of high school, teens can focus on subjects ranging from agriculture to the arts. They graduate with a *bachillerato* degree. They can also earn agricultural or technical degrees.

About 36 percent of students graduate from high school on schedule.

bachillerato
(ba-chee-yair-AH-toh)

Public or Private School?

Most students attend free public schools, but their experiences vary greatly. Since schools are often short on money, they often postpone repairs or building updates—for example, many rural schools are still without running water or power. They also pay their teachers low wages. To make enough money, teachers often work at several schools. They sometimes miss teaching a class because they cannot travel quickly enough between schools. To demand higher wages, public school teachers have stayed out of their classrooms and gone on strike.

Some rural schools only offer classes through the primary level. This makes it more difficult for older students to complete their education.

Some public schools are very demanding and competitive, especially those connected to the University of Buenos Aires. Students may spend a year preparing for the entrance exams to get accepted. Graduates from these elite schools have an advantage over other applicants to the university.

Most Argentine parents will send their children to private school if they can afford the high tuition, which ranges from 1,870 to 2,500 pesos (U.S.$600 to $800).

Since there is great demand for private schooling among upper-income families, more than 20 percent of all schools are private. One advantage of private school education is that students receive extensive language instruction. Public schools conduct their classes only in Spanish, Argentina's official language. They offer a foreign language, usually English, at a very basic level. Private schools, particularly those serving specific ethnic groups, offer instruction in English,

Siesta Time

Middle- and upper-income teens often do not work. After their school shift, they return home for the traditional rest period known as the siesta. However, the siesta is becoming rarer in some areas, particularly Buenos Aires. One teen remembers his siesta days:

It was so nice coming back from school, my mum used to wait for me with lunch ready. I ate and then [went] directly to bed, one or two hours. ... I think there are a lot of young people that sleep siesta, mostly the ones who still go to school in the country ... it's more like a ritual that shouldn't be disturbed.

Children need this rest since families eat dinner at 9 P.M. or later, and children may not go to bed until 11 P.M. While adults in busy cities have little time for this midday rest, in the countryside, shops and businesses still close in early afternoon for siesta time.

French, German, or Italian. There are also religious schools at every level—most prominently Catholic institutions and Jewish day schools.

Poverty's Challenge to Education

Although nearly all Argentine children complete elementary school, there are challenges to completing their secondary education. The poorest Argentine families struggle with unemployment and poverty. Though public schools are free, students must buy their uniforms and books and find transportation. The costs of having several children in school can burden a family. A single uniform costs around 110 pesos (U.S.$35). Low-income teens often leave school to work and help support their families.

School attendance is lowest in the country's rural interior. Most illiterate Argentines live in these areas. Some of these teens only attend school for a few years since they have to farm. Teens cannot legally work before age 14 unless they are working on farms or in family-run businesses. However, it is estimated that around 500,000 children below the age of 15 work, usually holding jobs in domestic service, making clothing or food, or collecting trash. To counter this, the country has installed harsh fines for employers who hire young workers. The penalty can range from 1,090 to 5,450 pesos (U.S$350 to $1,750) per child.

Rural teens live in communities on

desolate plains, mountains, or plateaus. They travel by foot, bicycle, or even horseback. They often cannot get to distant schools, particularly when rain turns unpaved roads to mud. In contrast, teens in highly populated Buenos Aires live within a half-hour of their schools. Landowners who run sprawling ranches sometimes educate their employees' children. They set up one-room schools on their property, supervised by a lone teacher. The quality of these schools varies and depends on the landowner's generosity.

More than 4,500 tons (4,050 metric tons) of garbage are generated daily in Buenos Aires. Collecting trash is one way children can make a living.

Rural public schools often suffer from a lack of funding compared with urban and suburban ones. This is caused by the country's distribution of wealth. Buenos Aires and other major cities get the most government school and transportation funding. Rural schools also vary among provinces, depending on what the area produces. Since market prices for beef and sugar are lower than for other products, for example, less money flows into the schools of the communities that sell them.

Yet the Argentine government has built thousands of small schools in remote provinces to teach adults to read and write. It tries to keep teens in school through the *jornada completa,* or full-day program. This doubles the length of the school day in grades seven to nine. Leaders hope that if students spend more time with teachers, they will be more likely to stay in school. The government also introduced the third school shift from 7 P.M. to 11 P.M. for teens who must work full time during the day.

jornada completa
(hor-NAH-thah cohm-PLAY-ta)

University Life

More and more Argentine youth are pursuing higher education. Almost half of high school graduates go on to a university. Students usually live at home and work while attending their local university. As in high school, night courses are popular with college students who work full time.

Students have many ways to

Lighting Up Schools With the Sun

Argentina's rural students often attend schools without electricity. This means no lights, computers, or any other modern technology. Since 1995, the government has been bringing solar energy to these remote schools. In the northeastern province of Corrientes, for example, the government is spending 6.2 million pesos (U.S.$2 million) for engineers to install solar cells on school roofs. Since 2005, this effort has brought solar power to 85 schools.

More than a million students enroll in university-level courses every year.

earn their degrees. There are 38 state universities and 31 private universities in the country. There are also six state and 13 private institutes, one provincial university, one foreign university, and one international university. Private universities usually draw upper-income students because of high tuition rates, which can be more than 31,140 pesos (U.S.$10,000) per year. They allow students to complete degrees one year sooner than public universities. They often have better facilities and organization. However, public universities offer some of the best education. People usually consider the University of Buenos Aires as South America's largest and most prestigious education center.

The most popular degrees are economics, communications, and management, followed closely by architecture and design, computer science, engineering, law, medicine, education, and psychology. Other teens choose to devote their education to the arts—such as music, theater, and fine arts—at institutes and conservatories. Those who are interested in subjects such as nursing, teaching, or business study at institutions focusing on their chosen area of study.

Buenos Aires is the second most populated city in South America (after São Paulo, Brazil) and the 10th most populated city in the world.

2

Diverse Lives

ARGENTINA'S PLAINS, PLATEAUS, FORESTS, AND MOUNTAINS FILL NEARLY THE ENTIRE SOUTHERN HALF OF SOUTH AMERICA. Yet almost 90 percent of its population lives in cities, making Argentina one of the world's most urbanized countries. About 13 million people, or one-third of the population, live in Buenos Aires and its suburbs. Urban teens lead different lifesyles. Some live in mansions; others have no running water. Still others sleep on the streets. For rural teens, Buenos Aires and cities such as Córdoba, Mendoza, and La Plata are magnets. They offer the hope of a better life in a place that bustles with activity 24 hours a day. The population is growing faster in urban areas, particularly Buenos Aires, than anywhere else in the country.

The differences in city housing reflect the growing gap between the well-off and those who struggle. A family's income determines the quality of its home. In Buenos Aires, the busy city center is full of high-rise apartments surrounded by both exclusive suburban neighborhoods and slums.

Buenos Aires is divided into 48 neighborhoods. The brightly colored neighborhood La Boca is home to many working-class families.

Upper- and Middle-Income Lives

Some upper-income urban families live in spacious brick houses with swimming pools. Some live in modern, glass-front apartments. Urban Argentine families usually have one or two children.

Apartment living is ideal for those with such small families. However, expenses such as rent and electricity can consume a large part of a middle-income family's money, and those who have extended families living with them often lack extra room and privacy.

High-end apartments usually have three bedrooms, allowing family members to have their own. In smaller cities and suburbs with more space, most wealthy families live in single-family homes.

Middle-class teens usually do not have many responsibilities at home. Families often hire maids to do the laundry, cook, and care for children. Instead, teens have time outside of school to take karate, dance, or tennis lessons, or meet their friends to play soccer at a sports club or playground.

Teens also enjoy chatting with their

The Economic Crisis Hit Hard

Though Argentina historically has been among the world's wealthiest countries, its economy has been unstable. Inflation makes it difficult for families to support themselves. Thirty years of inflation led to an economic crisis that peaked in December 2001. It affected nearly everyone in the country and the government itself.

To cover its enormous debts, Argentina borrowed billions of dollars from foreign countries. Later it could not pay them back. Economic growth slowed dramatically. Millions lost jobs as factories and other businesses closed. One quarter of the population was unemployed by the middle of 2002. For those who stayed employed, their average paycheck decreased by 20 percent between 1999 and 2002.

Argentines panicked. They tried to take money out of their bank accounts, but the government blocked their access. Under President Eduardo Duhalde, the value of the Argentine peso fell. Millions of people lost their life's savings almost overnight. One teen remembers the crisis:

It wasn't good. ... the prices went up so fast and we were desperate ... Lots of people had economic problems by that time. The prices were in the clouds and lots of people couldn't take their savings out of the bank, and if they could it was in pesos and not dollars ... it used to be one dollar, one peso, and then it was one dollar, three pesos, so you can imagine.

Nearly six in 10 people fell into poverty. Many lost their homes and could not afford food or clothing. Soup kitchens popped up on street corners. Since their money was virtually useless, people set up markets where they could trade their possessions for necessities. Protesters died in violent confrontations with police. Thousands of mostly young, well-educated people left the country, fleeing to places such as Italy and Spain. By 2002, the economy began to rebound.

The Buenos Aires neighborhood San Isidro is known for its beautiful houses and affluent residents. However, it is also known for La Cava, the largest slum in the city.

friends on the Internet. Nearly one-quarter of Argentines go online. This is the third highest number in South America, behind Brazil and Colombia. Teens can get online at home, at school, and at cafés. When heavy rains disrupt phone lines and electricity, which can happen all over the country, Argentines stay connected with cell phones.

Cities offer teens many ways to move about on their own. Driver's licenses can be obtained at 18, but it is uncommon for teens to have their own cars since most middle-income families cannot afford more than one vehicle. But teens can ride the subway or take the bus. Others can ride into town on air-conditioned commuter trains, hail one of Buenos Aires' 40,000 taxicabs, or walk. Pedestrians fill the sidewalks at nearly every hour of the day or night.

Life in the "Villas Miserias"

The poorest city-dwellers live in *villas miserias*, or towns of misery. These areas are filled with families most affected by the economic crisis of 2001. Migrants from neighboring countries such as Bolivia and Paraguay also end up here. They come to the cities looking for work. Alongside these migrants live Argentines who left the countryside for the same reason. These areas are already over-crowded. New arrivals now build shacks in empty inner-city lots.

Between 1950 and 2005, Argentina's urban population more than tripled, while its rural population

villas miserias
(VEE-yahs mee-sair-EE-ahs)

Shaped by Immigration

Several waves of immigration have shaped Argentina's culture. Students walking to school along the crowded Buenos Aires streets pass newsstands with newspapers in Italian, French, German, Portuguese, and Hebrew. They may say goodbye to each other with the Italian "Ciao!"

Buenos Aires residents are quite proud of their immigrant heritage. They call themselves *porteños*—or people of the port—since they live next to one of the world's busiest port. Some Jewish immigrants arrived as early as the 15th century to flee persecution in Spain and Portugal. The first large wave of immigrants, primarily European Jews and Italians, began arriving in Argentina in the 1880s. Spanish immigrants followed two decades later.

Koreans are the most recent addition to the diverse country. Because of immigration, the layout of Argentine cities often looks European. With wide, tree-lined streets, plazas, and parks with marble statues, Buenos Aires has been called the Paris of South America.

porteños
(por-TAY-nyos)

25

It has been estimated that between 300,000 and 500,000 of Buenos Aires' residents live in slums.

decreased by almost half. Thousands of these people live on the outskirts of Buenos Aires. Slums are the fastest growing parts of cities. There, people are crowded together in unstable shacks, often living more than three to a room. Families build their homes out of sheet metal, salvaged wood, bricks, and even cardboard. Rain turns the unpaved, garbage-filled streets to mud.

Few of these areas have sewer systems or electricity. A third of the population has no access to clean drinking water. They often suffer from illnesses because of these filthy living conditions. The infant mortality rate is nearly three times the national average.

The children of illegal immigrants in the villas face great odds. In the past, they were not allowed to attend

What's Paco?

In recent years, a new cheap drug has taken hold of young, lower-income Argentines. The drug, called *paco*, is a low-grade form of cocaine. Argentina is Latin America's largest consumer of the drug. People have blamed paco's growing popularity on economic troubles and its impact on the poor.

paco
(PAH-coh)

Paco is easy for young people to get in villas miserias. The drug flows in from neighboring cocaine-producing countries such as Bolivia. They can buy a dose at street stands for just 5 pesos (U.S.$1.50). Since the drug is highly addictive, users commit violent crimes to feed their habit. Police say the villas miserias are too dangerous for them to enter. Residents are often afraid to talk to police for fear of punishment by the drug rings.

Yet addicts' mothers have started to organize support groups for themselves and their children. One mother commented:

They [the addicts] swap food for drugs and then eat from bins. It rots their brains. Punishment doesn't work [because] the addict is sick, he can't help it.

public school because their parents were not legal, tax-paying workers. In 2003, Argentina approved a measure to allow the children of illegal immigrants the right to education and health care. However, an education is still not guaranteed. Without an education, people in the villas are not able to improve their lives. The fierce competition for jobs among the many well-educated

The nearly 800 crossing points along Argentina's 2,500-mile (4,000-kilometer) border makes controlling the entry of illegal immigrants difficult.

Argentines makes life even more difficult.

The residents of the villas miserias try to help themselves. They hold fundraisers to pay for basic utilities. Volunteer groups and churches raise money to build decent housing for slum residents. They also formed a national organization to pressure the government into funding health clinics and programs to deal with youth crime.

It appears that Argentina's recent economic recovery is trickling down to the slums. The country's record poverty level of 50 percent in 2001 fell to just under 25 percent by 2007. Paved roads and new public housing are appearing in the villas miserias.

For the *chicos de la calle,* or

chicos de la calle
*(CHEE-cohs
THAY LAH CAH-yay)*

street children, the future seems bleak. More than 3,000 young people, from infants to teens, live on the Buenos Aires streets. They sleep under freeways and in plazas. There are at least twice as many young people on the streets today as in 2001, when the economy collapsed. Some travel thousands of miles, leaving the countryside to escape the hunger, poverty, and abusive homes of unemployed parents. They arrive by one of the many train lines that end in Buenos Aires. Others leave their homes in the villas miserias for the same reasons.

These teens must care for themselves. They find their clothes in dumpsters. They beg, steal purses, juggle, and open cab doors for a few coins. They create their own families by forming gangs of up to 15 people. These *ranchadas* sleep in groups on filthy mattresses or cardboard. They pool their money to buy food

ranchadas
(rahn-CHAH-thahs)

and drugs. More than 90 percent of street children in Buenos Aires take illegal drugs such as paco. Their concerns are not on the future but on surviving the present. Tatiana, a 14-year-old who lives on the streets of Buenos Aires, says:

Sometimes I get very, very sad. And I can't eat. I can't sleep. I just lie here. What else is there to do?

Between 50 and 60 percent of the population fell into poverty after the economic crisis.

Rural Life

While many parts of Buenos Aires seem European, the sparsely populated rural areas beyond it look more like the rest of Latin America. Horses pull carts along cobblestone streets. Several members of a rural family might all balance on a bike or ride horses to get around town. Argentina's rural teens live in towns and on small farms on the central plains of the Pampas, in the north along the rugged Andes mountains, and on the bleak southern plateau of Patagonia. Since rural towns lie far apart and far from cities, people often travel by bus. However, rain can flood the dirt roads so only horse-drawn carts can pass.

The daily lives of the rural wealthy and poor are quite different, just as in the cities. Wealthy Argentines own *estancias*, or large farms, throughout the country. These farms have luxurious homes and may have swimming pools, tennis courts, and polo fields. Some very large estancias are like small

estancias
(ay-STAHN-see-ahs)

Estancias are a popular tourist destination, offering activities such as horseback riding, cattle drives, swimming, and hiking.

villages with their own chapels and schools. Sometimes part of the family will live in the city while their children attend school.

Estancias employ many farm workers. These rural people work long days and go to bed early. Some estancias have vineyards, orchards, and grain fields. Near Buenos Aires, there are cattle ranches. These ranches employ *gauchos,* or ranch hands, who rope cattle and break horses but also drive tractors and vaccinate cattle.

The streets of rural towns radiate from tree-lined squares. Single-family homes fill the towns and suburbs. Families of farm laborers live in small

gauchos
(GAU-chos)

Farmers protested the government's export tax increase from 27 percent to 45 percent in 2008. The tax applied to products such as beef, soybeans, and sunflower oil.

Common Names

Although Argentine names are commonly used, Buenos Aires' large Jewish population means that many traditional Hebrew names are used as well.

Nicknames are also used among friends and can be based on real or imaginary physical characteristics. A teen might call his friend *chancho* (like a pig), *gordo* (fat), or *che*, which means buddy or pal. Other traditional names, such as the Jewish name Moisés, have been changed to sound more modern (such as Mauricio, Marcos, or Mario).

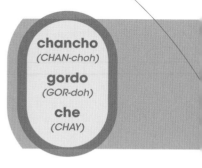

chancho
(CHAN-choh)

gordo
(GOR-doh)

che
(CHAY)

Common Argentine boys' names

Juan
Carlos
Jorge
José
Luis
Roberto
Alberto

Common Argentine girls' names

Maria
Ana
Marta
Susana
Alicia
Rosa

Common Jewish boys' names

David
Jacobo
Daniel
Jaime
Isaac
Ariel

Common Jewish girls' names

Ana
Raquel
Esther
Miriam
Perla
Támara

shacks. Families of farm owners and managers occupy bigger farmhouses, which are often painted white with red roofs. These homes are made of adobe, an inexpensive clay that retains heat. For homes in the frigid southern tip of Argentina, tanks of fuel arrive in horse-drawn carts to heat them.

Rural families tend to be larger than urban ones, having three or four children. Many of these families are lower-income and add on to their houses as they can afford to. When children marry and start their own families, they often build on to their parents' house and share a central patio.

Rural residents' lives center on working the land. Argentina's varied climate allows farmers to grow everything from sugarcane, bananas, grapes, and wheat to sheep and livestock. Young people spend much of their time outdoors, working or playing. Children care for animals and pick vegetables. They also help care for younger siblings or work at the family store. They learn to ride horses at an early age and even ride them to school. In their free time, small-town children may play in grassy parks. Young people also spend hours riding their bikes with friends.

Those living in the country often feel neglected by those who live in the cities. They think that while the cities are recovering from the economic crisis, their lives are still hard. Rural people still go hungry even though the country produces food for export.

Some indigenous people in the remote northern provinces have reportedly died of starvation. Illiteracy, unemployment, chronic disease, and poverty rates are also higher among indigenous people. Gabino Zambrara, vice president of an indigenous organization, said:

Our whole lives we've been waiting. We've spoken to many governments, to ministers, we've spoken to presidents. We've been asking every way you can think of, for our lands, for development, for our dignity. But we've not got them.

Thousands of rural residents have held demonstrations in Buenos Aires. They complain that they do not receive enough public money to improve education, health services, housing, and water supplies.

Argentines have more doctors per person than any other Latin American country. However, rural children suffer from a lack of access to health care. Children sometimes must travel hundreds of miles on foot or by cart to reach clinics. Passenger train service in most of the country stopped in 1993. Yet a train of volunteer doctors and dentists now makes rounds through the countryside. However, sometimes a rural community can wait up to a year for a visit. This may be the only time children in these areas get any medical attention.

Some of the poorest and most isolated groups in rural Argentina are the indigenous peoples. In other Latin American countries, they make up the majority of the population. However,

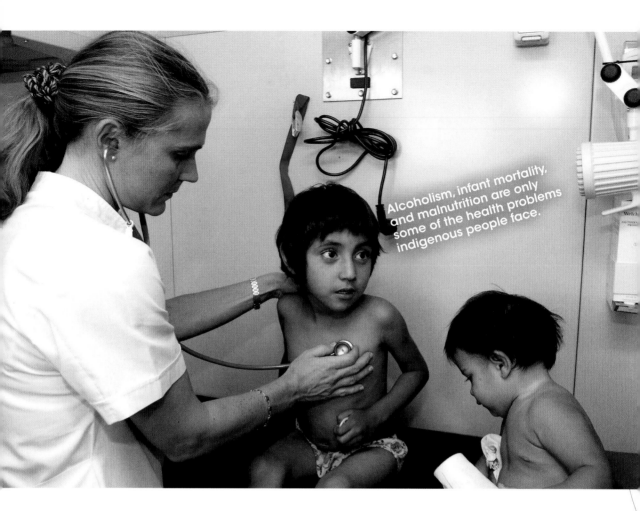

Alcoholism, infant mortality, and malnutrition are only some of the health problems indigenous people face.

97 percent of Argentina's population is Caucasian. Only 3 percent of the population is classified as "nonwhite"; indigenous people and *mestizos*, who have a mixture of both white and indigenous backgrounds, are included in this count. These people exist in such small numbers because diseases carried by European settlers killed many of their ancestors. The settlers also deliberately killed many people over the centuries. During the Indian Wars of 1870s and 1880s, for example, the native peoples living in the Pampas and in Patagonia were nearly wiped out. The settlers took their lands primarily for grazing cattle.

Along the Andes mountains,

mestizos
(may-STEE-sohs)

Argentina
Topographical
map

PACIFIC
OCEAN

BOLIVIA

Llullaillaco
Volcano

GRAN CHACO

PARAGUAY

Pilcomayo R.

FRONT RANGE

San Miguel
de Tucumán

Iguazú Falls

Iguazú R.

Catamarca

BRAZIL

Paraná R.

Mar Chiquita

Córdoba

Mt. Mercedario

Mt. Aconcagua

Mendoza

Rosario

Uruguay R.

URUGUAY

Buenos Aires

La Plata

Río de la Plata

Cape San Antonio

Salado R.

PAMPAS

Mar del Plata

Colorado R.

M
O
U
N
T
A
I
N
S

Negro R.

Lanín Volcano

Golfo San Matías

Valdés
Peninsula

ATLANTIC
OCEAN

A
N
D
E
S

CHILE

P
A
T
A
G
O
N
I
A

N
W   E
S

0   150   300 mi.
0   150   300 km

Golfo
San Jorge

Perito Moreno Glacier

Falkland Islands
(U.K.)

Lake Argentina

Bahía
Grande

West
Falkland

East
Falkland

Strait of
Magellan

CHILE

Isla Grande de
Tierra del Fuego

Isla de los
Estados

Ushuaia

Cape Horn

35

More than 60,000 indigenous people live in Chaco, the poorest province in Argentina.

indigenous communities lead challenging lives. They farm on mountain slopes and use llamas as pack animals. In the northwestern Gran Chaco region, development has driven away the animals they once hunted. Other indigenous groups live in the barren southern areas of Patagonia and Tierra del Fuego. Some people are worried that young indigenous people are not learning their community's native languages.

Young rural Argentines, indigenous or otherwise, are most likely to abandon the countryside for the cities. Those living in the country's most remote regions

feel the city's draw. Daniel Hofstatter, a parent and official of the remote town of Chorotis, has watched his town's population shrink. More than 800 of Argentina's small towns have virtually disappeared. He says young people are lured by city life as portrayed on television. Those left behind in rural communities often face few job opportunities and even hunger.

Meals and Sobremesa

Eating and drinking are social occasions for Argentines. Whether it is a multicourse dinner, a snack in a café, or tea, everyone enjoys *sobremesa*. The phrase literally means "over the table" and describes the tradition of staying to talk after a meal. Waiters do not hurry diners away once they have cleared the plates. Even fast-food restaurants such as McDonald's have remodeled so their customers can linger after their meals.

sobremesa
(soh-bray-MAY-sah)

Argentines celebrate most any event with an *asado,* or barbeque. Many people have home stoves designed with a *bifera* between the burners for grilling meat. Most every house with a patio or garden will have a grill, and grilled meat is also commonly sold at roadside stands. Asados often take place on the weekend when family and

asado
(ah-SAH-thoh)

bifera
(bee-FAIR-ah)

Popular items to grill are beef, lamb, pork, goat, chicken, and organ meats such as tripe, blood sausage, kidneys, and sweetbreads.

friends can gather.

Argentines eat more beef than nearly any country in the world. More cattle live in Argentina than people. Fifty-four million beef cattle live on the fertile plains of the Pampas region, so beef is inexpensive. Millions of sheep graze in Patagonia. This makes mutton the centerpiece of asados in the south. Argentines enjoy sirloin steak, known as *bife de chorizo*. They like empanadas, with the filling baked into a turnover of dough. Restaurants serve a simple steak called *churrasco* and one topped with fried egg called *bife a caballo*, or beef on horseback. Argentines

bife de chorizo
(BEE-fay THAY choh-REE-soh)
churrasco
(choo-RAHS-coh)

Chatting Over a Bowl of Maté

The most popular drink in Argentina is a tea called *maté*. Originally gauchos imitated the way Guaraní Indians made tea from the maté plant. This hollylike plant grows in the northeastern Mesopotamia region. The tea's caffeine lift once helped gauchos ride a long time without eating or sleeping. Today most Argentines drink maté several times a day.

Sharing maté is a ritual. Drinkers pour hot water over maté leaves in a bowl called a *bombilla*. They then sip the tea through a metal straw and pass it around. Maté tastes bitter, so younger children usually do not drink it. Maté is usually served plain, but can be sweetened with sugar or flavored with orange peel. While traditional bombillas are made from a hollow gourd, others are now made of wood or even silver.

maté
(MAH-tay)
bombilla
(bohm-BEEH-yah)

eat nearly every part of the cow, including the udder, intestines, heart, and tongue. Many restaurants even offer *asado con cuero*, an entire steer roasted with its hide and hair.

bife a caballo
(BEE-fay-AH cah-BAH-yoh)

asado con cuero
(ah-SAH-thoh COHN CWAY-roh)

Some Argentines also enjoy lasagna and ravioli, reflecting their Italian roots. (There are more than 1.5 million Italian speakers throughout the country, making it the second-most spoken language after Spanish.) Pasta is a popular dish because it is inexpensive and filling.

Argentines generally favor meat dishes over vegetables, but they do enjoy fruit. Since Argentina's land ranges from frigid to temperate to subtropical, a variety of fruits is available. These include apricots, cherries, grapes, peaches, pears, plums, and quinces. Apples from the Río Negro region are popular, as are the oranges, grapefruit, and tangerines from farmlands in the Mesopotamia region.

Argentines gather many times a day to eat and socialize. Breakfast is often a simple meal of *café con leche*, or coffee with milk, and croissants or yogurt. Many urban teens prefer to sleep

café con leche
(cah-FAH COHN LAY-chay)

until the last moment and skip breakfast entirely. Rural families eat a more hearty breakfast, often with meat. A mid-morning snack of maté and empanadas sustains people until lunch.

Argentines traditionally gather at home around 1 P.M. for lunch, followed by a siesta. Rural cooks might carry a clay pot with a stew of potatoes, beef, and corn called *carbonada* to workers in the field. Rural Argentines also eat *locro*, a stew of corn, beans, meat, and pumpkins, all common ingredients in the Andes regions. In wealthier homes, maids prepare large lunches of meat and vegetables.

carbonada
(cahr-boh-NAH-dah)

locro
(LOH-croh)

Dinner, the day's main meal, is not served until at least 9 P.M., and sometimes much later. So around 5 P.M., Argentines have an afternoon snack. Students returning from an afternoon school shift might have milk and a sandwich. They also may stop by one of the *confiterías*, or tearooms, found on nearly every city block. A favorite teatime dessert is a *factura*, a croissantlike pastry.

confiterías
(cohn-fee-tay-REE-ahs)

factura
(fahk-TOO-rah)

Around 10 P.M., the family will

Dinner is the one time of day when the whole family is together.

gather for a several-course dinner. The mood at the table is lively. Everyone talks about politics, sports, movies, and their days. Families also enjoy eating dinner out, often at sidewalk pizzerias. They have continued to do so even during hard economic times.

Teens' tastes often differ from their parents'. Children enjoy eating Italian-inspired dishes such as veal Parmesan and potato dumplings in a tomato and meat sauce. Teens also enjoy pizza and

Stands selling spicy sausage sandwiches known as choripán, burgers, and carbonated drinks are found throughout the country.

hamburgers. They drink soft drinks, lemonade, grapefruit-flavored tonic water, and coffee with milk. A popular drink among children is *liquado*, a thick fruit juice blended with milk or water. Teens find fast-food stands in malls affordable. All-you-can-eat restaurants are especially popular. Street stalls always have a variety of favorite foods.

Urban families shop once a week at large supermarkets. Yet many people prefer the fresh food available daily at traditional farmers' markets. During times of economic trouble, these vendors offered special payment arrangements so that more people could afford food. Shoppers also stop at various specialty stores, such as the bakery or butcher. *Galletiterías* are shops that sell only crackers and cookies. Other stores sell Italian pasta and sauces, German chocolates, and other specialty foods that appeal to Argentines with an immigrant heritage. In the country, traveling vendors knock on doors selling vegetables, fruits, and milk from horse-drawn carts.

liquado
(lee-KWA-thoh)

choripán
(cho-ri-PAN)

galletiterías
(gah-yay-tee-tay-REE-ahs)

Fathers were traditionally the heads of families while mothers were in charge of household duties. However, recently there has been an increase in women in the work force.

3

A Network of Friends and Family

ARGENTINES LOVE TO TALK, SHARE OPINIONS, AND DEBATE. They do this in the dining room, at restaurants, on buses, and along sidewalks. Family life is a favorite topic. Young people play a central role in the family and their culture. When they first meet, they ask each other many questions about their families. Strangers stop to fuss over babies. Adults take children everywhere they go at whatever time. From an early age, children learn to say what they think and join in adult discussions.

Family size varies throughout the country. Urban families are usually small, with one or two children. Extended-family members often live nearby. Grandparents, uncles, aunts, and cousins gather for weddings, baptisms, parties, and holidays. In the countryside, families tend to have three or more children. Sometimes grandparents, uncles, and aunts live in the same home. A child's parents

43

Mothers play important roles in their childrens' lives.

padrinos
(pa-THREE-nohs)

will choose godparents, or *padrinos,* at his or her birth. They offer guidance. They shower children with gifts, affection, and advice, just like relatives. Parties, outings, and meals offer teens and young children in Argentina many opportunities to socialize with older family members. Children play and socialize with cousins who are often among their best friends. Family members rely on each other. They lend money or tools and care for children or sick relatives.

The extended family helps raise children to adulthood. This happens whether they live under the same roof or in different parts of the same city. In Argentina, children become adults at age 21. They usually live in their parents' houses until they marry. They live by their families' rules and are influenced by their decisions. Even older teens and university students rely on their families. Family members use connections to help them get into good schools and land jobs. Young married couples usually find housing close to their parents.

Changing Gender Roles

Women historically have tended to the home and family. Men were the authority figures and primary income-earners. Today more than half of urban women work. Most young Argentines believe women have the right to a career as well as a marriage and family. Yet many still consider the home to be under the control of

Body Language

Argentines use their entire bodies when they talk. They move their hands and arms as they speak. They also stand close while talking. They will even grab the listener's arm to make a point. When Argentines enter a crowded room, they greet everyone. They shake hands and kiss the cheeks of friends and strangers alike. Women kiss each other once on the right cheek. Once men know each other, they also may kiss each other on the cheek. This practice began as an act of rebellion in the mid-1980s after the military decided that kissing was affection that men should not show each other.

As more Argentine women gain jobs and careers, some men find themselves in an unfamiliar role.

the mother, with the father's opinion holding great weight there.

Argentina's divorce rate is the highest in South America. This changing dynamic is altering the country's traditional family structure. Children usually live with their mothers after a divorce. Many such children feel pressured to find jobs and contribute to the household. Since many mothers work outside the home, these children often spend many hours on their own.

Time With Friends

Friends are very important to Argentine teens. They often make them through school and sports clubs. Together they go out in groups to favorite hangouts and enjoy meeting at restaurants to drink sodas, eat French fries, and talk about dating, music, and poetry. Dancing at discos is a popular form of entertainment. Some of these discos can hold several thousand people. Some are decorated with themes from comics and video games.

Free to Choose

Buenos Aires is the most open and free community in Latin America. In 2002, it became the first city to recognize the civil unions of same-sex couples—although it does not use the term marriage. There are restaurants, bars, movie theaters, clubs, and hotels that cater to same-sex clients. Around one-fifth of Argentine tourists are gay. But there is no traditional gay neighborhood—instead, it is becoming an accepted way of life. Some credit this to Argentina's rising economic power of the early 1990s. As one Buenos Aires resident explains:

People traveled and found there were other ways of living that were completely different than what they were used to.

Argentines make an effort to look well groomed. Both men and women pay special attention to their hair, skin, and nails. Upper-income teens keep up with the latest global fashions that they see in television ads and magazines. Today some are turning toward a more personal style. They might hunt through second-hand stores and mix old and new clothing together in a unique way. Others simply wear leather jackets and comfortable shoes.

Being Beautiful

Looking good is important in Argentina. Women and girls are sometimes humiliated in clothing shops when salespeople tell them they don't carry their size. Television and magazine advertisements are full of images of beautiful, thin people. Many young girls, and some young boys, spend money and take great effort to look like these models. About a quarter of girls—and a smaller number of boys—struggle with an obsession with weight loss and eating disorders such as anorexia. Plastic surgery is not an uncommon graduation gift. In response, a law requires clothing manufacturers to make clothing in larger sizes and stores to display a range of sizes.

Buenos Aires has a reputation as one of the best shopping spots in Latin America.

47

Thousands of members of murgas, dancing, drumming, and singing groups, perform during Carnival.

4

Celebrating Throughout the Year

CROWDS CHEER AND FIREWORKS EXPLODE AT MIDNIGHT AS EACH NEW YEAR ARRIVES IN BUENOS AIRES. Cars draped with colorful banners go through the streets, honking. Friends and families gather to eat and dance. Young people stay up late and throw confetti at each other. Religious and cultural holidays throughout the year give Argentines many excuses to celebrate with food, family, and music at home or in places of worship.

More than 90 percent of Argentines consider themselves Roman Catholic, and most celebrate holidays such as Christmas and Easter. Although fewer than 20 percent attend church, Argentines demonstrate their faith in other ways. They may make the sign of the cross when they pass a church or carry a card with a saint's portrait for protection.

Though most Argentines embrace Catholicism, others practice a variety of religions. In some parts of

murga
(MOOR-gah)

49

the countryside, rural Argentines hold celebrations mixing Catholicism with indigenous religions. Every city has its own synagogue, since 2 percent of the population is Jewish. Argentina is home to the largest Jewish community in Latin America. Other cities house Muslims, Protestants, and Mormons.

Urban teens usually are less involved in religious services and celebrations than their rural peers. On religious holidays, city teens may share a special lunch or dinner with their families before meeting their friends at discos. Yet many holidays offer teens, both in the city and countryside, a chance to have fun and even make mischief.

Pilgrimages and Roadside Shrines

Most Argentines eventually make the pilgrimage to the chapel of the Virgen de Luján. A church stands where, in 1630, a statue of the Virgin Mary tumbled out of a wagon and the oxen refused to go on. More than 4 million pilgrims visit each year. Some even make the 40-mile (64-km) trip from Buenos Aires on foot.

Rural Argentines also make offerings at roadside shrines. Argentines stop along highways to place water bottles to celebrate the sacrifice of La Difunta Correa, or The Dead Correa. The story goes that a woman from the Correa family and her baby were lost in the desert. The woman died of thirst. However, rescuers found her baby had survived by nursing. People at the shrines pray for safe travels and good fortune in their business, relationships, and health. When the water evaporates, they believe La Difunta Correa has drunk. The Catholic Church disapproves and considers the practice superstitious.

Arab and Southeast Asian immigrants brought Islam to Argentina.

Religions

Experts disagree on the number of Jewish people residing in Argentina. However, the average numbers tend to be between 200,000 and 300,000.

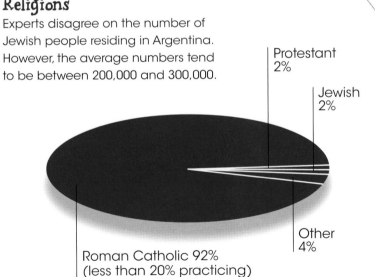

Protestant 2%

Jewish 2%

Other 4%

Roman Catholic 92% (less than 20% practicing)

Source: The United States Central Intelligence Agency. *The World Factbook—Argentina.*

Carnival

Argentines celebrate Carnival in various ways throughout the country over a long weekend in February. These parties occur just before Ash Wednesday, the beginning of Lent. Roman Catholics around the world make personal sacrifices during this time, giving up favorite things in the days before Easter.

Carnival is the last summer holiday for students in the Southern Hemisphere before the school year begins. Costumes are planned up to a year in advance. They dress like kings and queens, witches, animals, clowns, and cartoon characters. They spray fake snow and

The biggest and most important Carnival celebrations occur in Gualeguaychú.

Calendar of Holidays

Año Nuevo (New Year's Day)

January 1

Viernes Santo (Good Friday)

Friday before Easter

Día de la Memoria por la Verdad y la Justicia (Truth and Justice Day)

March 24; honors the victims of the military dictatorship of 1976–1983

Día del Veterano y los Caídos en la Guerra de Malvinas (Malvinas Day)

April 2; commemorates veterans of the Falklands War

Día del Trabajador (Labor Day)

May 1

Revolución de Mayo (Anniversary of the Revolution of 1810)

May 25

Día de la Bandera (Flag Day)

June 10

Día de la Independencia (Independence Day)

July 9

Día del Libertador José de San Martín (Anniversary of the death of General José de San Martín)

Third Monday in August

Día de la Raza (Columbus Day)

October 12

Día de la Inmaculada Concepción (Immaculate Conception Day)

December 8

Día de Navidad (Christmas)

December 25

launch water balloons from rooftops at friends and strangers. Girls aim for boys, and boys aim for girls.

Argentines generally do not celebrate Carnival on the scale of the neighboring country of Brazil. Nevertheless, celebrations in rural provinces can be grand. People decorate towns with colorful banners. They close roads to cars as parades of floats pass by. People beating bass drums called *bombos* dance while carrying sprigs of sweet basil. Children wear masks with glass eyes, feathers, and pieces of mirror. Everyone gathers under colorful tents to eat corn stew and dance the *zamba* with twirling handkerchiefs.

bombos
(BOHM-bohs)

zamba
(SAHM-bah)

The Corsódromo in Gualeguaychú seats 350,000 people and has room for 700 dancers onstage.

Christmas

On Christmas Eve, families may eat outside on patios or in air-conditioned houses as late as 11:30 P.M. Families eat cold beef or chicken, fruit salad, and iced tea. Then they share plates of almonds, dried fruits, and *pan dulce*, a sweet bread with raisins and nuts. Relatives drop by. Everyone opens gifts, and children are allowed to stay up late. The next day is spent quietly at home with the family.

pan dulce
(PAHN DOOL-say)

Argentine children look forward to the visit of Los Tres Reyes Magos, or the Three Kings, on January 6. Families set out a Nativity scene under a tree. It is usually artificial and decorated with lights and cotton balls for snow. The Nativity figures represent the animals and people present at the manger the

Because Christmas in Argentina occurs in the summer, gift-giving and tree-decorating are joined by picnics and fireworks.

night Jesus was born. As January 6 approaches, the figures of the Three Kings bearing gifts are moved closer to the baby. The night before the holiday, the figures are standing next to Jesus. Children leave their shoes out for the Three Kings to fill with gifts.

Honoring the Dead

Roman Catholicism and indigenous beliefs influence Argentines' relationships with the dead. They celebrate, honor, and connect with the dead through rituals. A family will often spend an afternoon visiting a cemetery where family tombs crowd together along narrow streets. They may buy coffee from vendors or have a picnic. They lay fresh flowers on the graves of loved ones or famous people such as political leaders and musicians.

Celebrating Argentina

Argentines celebrate every aspect of their culture, from their dances to their crops to their foods. During the National Immigrant Festival in September, residents of the province of Misiones build a neighborhood of model houses. These represent the cultures that shaped Argentina. Visitors sample foods and hear music inside typical houses from England, Italy, Switzerland, Germany, Japan, and France. Young people dress in the clothing of their ancestors and perform European folk dances such as the Irish jig and the Polish polka. Musicians

The "Disappeared"

A somber event has taken place each Thursday since 1977 in Buenos Aires' Plaza de Mayo. In sight of the presidential Casa Rosada palace, a group of women gathers. They wear white scarves and carry photographs of young men and women. People call these mothers the Madres de la Plaza de Mayo. They march to demand that the government explain what happened to their children. On the plaza floor, people have painted silhouettes symbolizing the missing loved ones known as *los desaparecidos*, or "the disappeared."

Between 1976 and 1983, Lieutenant General Jorge Rafael Videla was in charge of the government. During El Proceso, or "The Process," military rulers arrested anyone suspected of opposing Videla. Most of those arrested were young adults and students from middle-income backgrounds.

In 1976, Ibérico St. Jean, the

los desaparecidos
(lohs dehs-ah-pah-reh-SEE-thos)

governor of Buenos Aires, described the mission of El Proceso:

First we will kill all the subversives, then we will kill their collaborators, then ... their sympathizers, then ... those who remain indifferent; and finally, we will kill the timid.

The three main groups of people punished were Jews, gays, and women. They were jailed and tortured with beatings and electrical shocks. An estimated 20,000 to 30,000 Argentine citizens disappeared during this period, which is now called the "Dirty War." Most people assume they were murdered or died in jail. The mothers marching today say they do so for a larger purpose. They wish to bring attention to "discrimination of any form."

The Madres de la Plaza de Mayo were nominated for a Nobel Prize in 1980, and again in 2008.

and antique carriages bearing flags of various countries parade down the streets. The community selects a national queen. To be nominated for this position, the candidate must be fluent in her ancestors' native language and must also know how her country has contributed to Argentina's history.

Gaucho culture has influenced the Argentine people so much that it is celebrated during the National Gaucho Festival in Buenos Aires. Boys dress in traditional gaucho clothing, and girls dress in long skirts and wear their hair down like *chinas*, the women who lived with the gauchos. Poetry contests and folk dances are major parts of the celebration. During folk dances such as the *zapatéo*, dancers stomp their feet, clap their hands, and clack the gaucho weapon, the *boleadora,* to keep time.

chinas
(CHEE-nahs)

zapatéo
(sah-pah-TAY-oh)

Argentines also celebrate their most beloved foods. The wine-producing mountain town of Vendimia hosts the Grape Festival every year. A priest blesses the vines, and the town chooses a festival queen. A parade includes young people on decorated bicycles and carts filled with grapes. Other festivals that celebrate food are the Harvest of the Fish in coastal Mar del Plata and the Snow Festival in Bariloche. During the Harvest of the Fish, people eat seafood and dress as sea creatures. The queen of the sea leads a parade while riding in a shell. A parade of skis takes place at night by torchlight at the Snow Festival, and a queen of chocolate is crowned.

boleadora
(boh-lay-ah-THO-rah)

After more than 400 years, the gaucho culture is still alive and well.

Collecting trash is just one way some Argentine teens help support their famillies and earn extra money.

5 Hoping for Work

WHEN ARGENTINES ARE FRUSTRATED, THEY LET THE GOVERNMENT KNOW. They march in the streets banging pots and pans. During the economic crisis of 2001 and 2002, more than half the country fell into poverty. Today's teens remember their parents' losing jobs and life savings. They recall their families' struggle to buy food and other necessities.

During this stressful time, some lower- and middle-income teens committed robberies. Some painted graffiti on city walls. Many from the countryside left homes where there was not enough to eat and became street children. Others took part in demonstrations at the National Congress.

Argentina has regained its place as one of South America's wealthiest countries. Yet many teens remain wary about their future in the job market. Argentina has seen periods of economic growth, followed by economic problems. Since 2003, Argentina's economy has mostly recovered. Unemployment has fallen. Argentina's many resources continue to create wealth and jobs. Food crops are plentiful. Petroleum

Nearly 50 percent of all children in Argentina live in poverty.

reserves provide all the energy the country needs and some for export. Its well-educated work force numbers more than 16 million.

Pressure to Work

Before the economic crisis, Argentina was unique in Latin America because it had a large middle class. Today middle-income families still feel economic pressures. Unemployment has fallen from 25 percent in 2002 to less than 15 percent. Yet inflation persists. The national minimum wage is 980 pesos (U.S.$315), yet this is still more than 10 percent less than a family of four needs to maintain a decent standard of living. So parents work longer or multiple shifts to support their families.

Middle-income teens are dependent on their parents. They want to find jobs to help their families and earn spending money. In fact, a survey found that 60 percent of teens believe education is necessary to finding secure jobs. This is difficult since lower- and middle-income youths usually do not have access to a car. Free university education means there are plenty of well-educated people around. So teens must compete fiercely for jobs. Many teens create their own, such as washing cars or walking dogs. They also become *trabajadores de fin de semana,* the weekend workers who head to downtown neighborhoods and suburban plazas to be clowns, mimes, and jugglers working for change from passersby. Local governments also fund theater troupes that put on performances and parades.

Competition for Low-End Jobs

Argentines must compete for lower-income jobs with each other and with at least 200,000 immigrants working illegally in the country. Most come from Bolivia, Peru, and Paraguay. These immigrants can earn more money and have better lifestyles in Argentina

trabajadores de fin de semana
(trah-bah-hah-THO-rays THEY FEEN THEY say-MAH-nah)

Middle- and upper-income teens may spend their time volunteering rather than working.

Employment

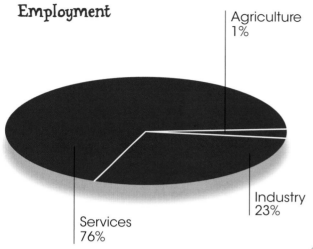

Agriculture
1%

Industry
23%

Services
76%

Source: The United States Central Intelligence Agency. *The World Factbook—Argentina.*

than in their own countries and are willing to work illegally. Some estimate that 30 percent of Argentina's work force is paid in cash and pays no taxes.

These workers perform manual labor such as ditch digging and construction work. They also work in meatpacking, milling, and textile factories in the large cities. They may work in miserable conditions without any health care or vacation

There is some disagreement about the number of illegal immigrants in Argentina. Some estimate that there may be as few as 200,000, while others put the number closer to 1 million.

Agriculture accounts for more than one-third of all employment in Argnetina.

time. Immigrant women often work as maids in middle- and upper-income Argentine homes. They often earn less than the country's minimum wage. Argentines respect them for their hard work but also resent them for taking away jobs.

Work in the countryside is harder to find. Unemployment and hunger in rural areas have risen. This comes as large commercial farms of soybeans, for example, replace smaller, family-run farms that once raised cotton, tobacco, and food crops. This results in unemployment since smaller farms need about one worker for every 20 acres (8 hectares), while the large, commercial farms need only one worker for every 500 acres (200 hectares). Large farms do not have as many tractors or special farming equipment as do farms in other developed countries. They rely heavily

Argentina
Land use map

BOLIVIA

PARAGUAY

Llamas
Goats
•Salta

Cattle

San Miguel
de Tucumán
Resistencia
•
Catamarca•
Santiago
del Estero•
Corrientes

Cattle
Sheep

BRAZIL

PACIFIC
OCEAN

San
Juan•
Córdoba•
Santa
Fe•

URUGUAY

Mendoza•
Rosario•

Hogs

Buenos Aires•
La Plata•
Río de la Plata

Cattle

ATLANTIC
OCEAN

Goats

Bahía
Blanca•
Mar del Plata•

Sheep

Valdés
Peninsula

N
W   E
S

0   150   300 mi.
0   150   300 km

Sheep

Land Use

Forest
Livestock
Manufacturing
Tropical crops
Wheat and corn
Nonagricultural land

Falkland Islands
(U.K.)

CHILE
Sheep
•Ushuaia

on thousands of workers from neighboring countries such as Bolivia, Peru, and Paraguay to supplement the machines they do have for planting and harvesting.

Unemployed Argentines living in the slums will sometimes form picket lines and block roads. They carry signs calling for more jobs and better social services. Lower-income teens have a hard time finding jobs, particularly without a high school degree.

Unemployment drives entire families from the villas miserias to roam the city, collecting trash to sell at recycling centers. An estimated 30,000 to 40,000 of these *cartoneros*, or "people of the cardboard," roam the city streets each evening. They will take their finds to be sold at recycling

cartoneros
(cahr-toh-NAY-rohs)

More than half of all cartoneros are children.

centers. They earn between 10 and 15 pesos a day (U.S.$3 and $5). This is often their only source of income.

More Opportunities for Women

More than one-third of today's labor force is female. Yet young Argentine women face challenges. They often are paid less than men and are given fewer opportunities to advance in the workplace. Fewer than 10 percent of managers and 12 percent of executives in large companies are women.

However, young women feel confident about finding their place in the economy. Half of university students

Eva Perón, Hero of the Poor

The face of Eva Perón, the woman adoring Argentines called Evita, still appears in portraits in people's homes and on political posters. She ran away from her rural home to Buenos Aires in the 1930s at age 15. After living in poverty, she became a popular radio actress. At 24, she married Juan Domingo Perón, an army colonel. When he was elected president in 1946, she became one of the most influential women in Argentine history.

Perón appealed to poor Argentines who struggled to survive when a small minority controlled the country's wealth. Sporting elegant dyed blond hair and fashionable clothes, she gave money, bicycles, and sewing machines to the poor. She avoided wealthy women who ran charities and started her own. It offered free health care and education for those who needed it. She was celebrated as the champion of the working classes.

When she died at 33 from cancer, a half-million mourners lined up to touch her coffin. Her epitaph in the cemetery reads, "Don't cry for me, Argentina, I remain quite near you." Today visitors still leave fresh flowers on her grave.

Cristina Fernández de Kirchner's husband, Néstor Kirchner, served as Argentina's president in 2003–2007.

are female. They go on to careers in law and medicine. Argentina elected its first female president, Cristina Fernández de Kirchner, in October 2007. She won by a wide margin, receiving nearly twice the number of votes as her nearest competitor. One official commented:

Cristina Fernández, in my view, is going to add something new to Argentina. ... In meeting her, it was obvious how interested she was in learning about foreign relations, and how curious intellectually she was about serious problems in this region.

New Opportunities, New Places

The economic crisis caused more than 250,000 young people to leave the country between 2000 and 2003. Around 10,000 Argentine Jews left the country during the crisis to start their lives over in Israel. Many were university graduates. Those who have returned hope they can find satisfactory work in Argentina—but they also have their doubts.

Teens understand that some traditional rules still apply when searching for jobs. They know that personal con-

BOLIVIA

PARAGUAY

JUJUY

San Salvador
de Jujuy

Salta
SALTA

CHACO

FORMOSA

Formosa

San Miguel
de Tucumán

TUCUMÁN

Santiago
del Estero

Resistencia

Corrientes

Posadas

MISIONES

CATAMARCA

Catamarca

SANTIAGO
DEL ESTERO

CORRIENTES

BRAZIL

LA RIOJA

SANTA
FE

SAN
JUAN

CÓRDOBA

San Juan

Córdoba

Santa
Fe

ENTRE
RÍOS

Paraná

URUGUAY

PACIFIC
OCEAN

Mendoza

Río
Cuarto

Rosario

San Luis

CHILE

MENDOZA

SAN
LUIS

Buenos Aires

La Plata

Río de la Plata

Santa Rosa

BUENOS AIRES

LA PAMPA

NEUQUÉN

Bahía
Blanca

Mar del Plata

Neuquén

RÍO NEGRO

ATLANTIC
OCEAN

Viedma

Valdés
Peninsula

Rawson

CHUBUT

N
W   E
S

Population Density
(People per square km)

0   150   300 mi.

0   150   300 km

	Greater than 100
	50–100
	10–49
	1–9
	Fewer than 1

SANTA CRUZ

Falkland Islands
(U.K.)

Río Gallegos

TIERRA DEL FUEGO

CHILE

Ushuaia

There are more than 600 vineyards in Mendoza.

nections help as much as education. Most Argentines find jobs in the service industry. Others work for the government and military or in banks, hospitals, restaurants, or schools. However, today's teens complain that school focuses too much on reading and memorization, and not enough on technology. They would like to be better prepared to compete for jobs in computer programming and graphic design.

A land of opportunity has opened on the cold, vast southern plateau of Patagonia. Oil derricks have joined the enormous herds of sheep that traditionally have been the area's greatest resource. Jobs in the energy and tourism industries are drawing people. Travelers from all over the world flock to Patagonia by the thousands. They hike, climb, and ski in its 19 national parks. This creates many new service jobs in hotels and restaurants.

The government has offered money to businesses if they move to Patagonia and create jobs. The government is also encouraging people to resettle in this area by lowering the taxes paid by those living there.

People from all over Buenos Aires gather at the Obelisk, one of the most popular celebration sites for soccer fans.

6

In Pursuit of Fun

el paseo
(ehl pah-SAY-oh)

ARGENTINES ARE AS LIKELY TO MEET UP WITH FRIENDS AT NOON AS AT MIDNIGHT. They enjoy activities such as dancing in clubs, joining the chaotic mobs of fans at soccer games, or rushing down a polo field on horseback. Quieter pleasures involve strolling and shopping with friends or sitting together at an outdoor café.

Strolling the Streets

Argentines' incomes determine what sort of fun they can afford. Yet *el paseo*, or strolling, is free. A common occurrence in rural areas, walking around a town or city square to see and be seen is an important event. Friends circle a square many times on foot. They might window shop or stop for a drink. In frigid Patagonia, friends circle plazas in their cars.

Argentines enjoy giving each other gifts. They wrap and tie even small gifts with ribbons. Because of recent economic troubles, shops allow customers to pay for these presents in installments.

71

An Old Gathering Place, With a Twist

Argentines are proud of being well read. Buenos Aires is teeming with bookstores. Some are open 24 hours a day. Argentina has produced many world-famous writers, such as Jorge Luis Borges and Julio Cortázar.

Teens enjoy visiting literary salons known as *salones literarios*. These places have enjoyed a revival since their popularity in the 1880s. Young people gather in these candlelit, book-filled rooms to sip a drink, read their poetry, or play music on stage. Today's salon has merged with the Internet café, so teens can chat with their friends online as well.

salones literarios
(sah-LOH-nehs lee-teh-RAH-ree-ohs)

All-Night Outings

Argentine shops close on Saturday afternoons as many people head home to rest up for Saturday night. Argentines might meet at a restaurant for a late dinner. Then they might dance at a disco until early morning and have coffee at dawn. Finally they return home and sleep until Sunday afternoon.

For Argentine youth, dancing is the evening's focus. They enjoy music from American and European bands. They also dance to music that combines old and new forms. Their national rock music, *rollingas*, is a style of dance

rollingas
(roh-ZHIN-gahs)

and song popular with young people throughout South America since the 1980s. It is influenced by heavy metal, country, reggae, Brazilian bossa nova, and tango. The 100-year-old music form tango is growing popular with teens. In clubs they dance to tangos mixed with electronic music. Today's middle- and upper-income teens have

Dance clubs are popular and inexpensive places for teens, with entrance fees between 6 and 9 pesos (U.S.$2 and $3).

Dancing to the Sounds of Melancholy

In Argentina's world-famous tango, a couple takes dramatic, sweeping steps across the *milonga*, the tango hall. The man wears a suit and neck scarf. The woman wears an elegant dress, high heels, and fishnet stockings. He leads her into each set of steps by pressing his hand on her back. Musicians play violins, pianos, and guitars. The *bandoneón*, an accordionlike instrument, gives the music its characteristic melancholic sound. Singers add mournful lyrics about hard lives and lost loves.

milonga
(meeh-LOHN-gah)

bandoneón
(bahn-doh-neh-OHN)

Tango developed among Buenos Aires' low-income residents in the 1880s. Its lyrics traditionally were in the local *lunfardo* dialect, which mixed the languages of its immigrants. In 1917, legendary tango singer Carlos Gardel sang before an audience of high-society Argentines at the Esmeralda Theater in Buenos Aires. His performance marked the universal acceptance of what some Argentines had considered unsophisticated.

lunfardo
(loon-FAHR-thoh)

Today's teens are rediscovering tango. They take classes and dance in outdoor plazas, homes, and tango halls. A radio station called Solo Tango plays tango exclusively. Each January, the National Tango Festival features performances with live musicians and dancers in front of audiences who dance their own tangos.

cumbias villeras
(KOOM-bee-yahs bee-YAIR-ahs)

embraced music styles such as *cumbias villeras*, which comes from low-income groups in Argentina's provinces.

Getting Out of Town

During weekends or vacations, urban Argentines seek out each other's company. Young people visit local parks with swimming pools, picnic areas, small zoos, and hand-cranked carousels. They might head to shopping malls or visit relatives with their families.

Beach towns along the Atlantic coast fill with millions of vacationers during summer vacation in January and February, and again during the three-week school holiday in July. Exclusive beach resorts catering to the wealthy have cropped up around fishing villages. Each year, as many as 6 million people, many of them middle-class families and students, swamp the beach resort of Mar del Plata, 250 miles (400 km) south of Buenos Aires.

Argentines enjoy the countryside differently, depending on how much money they have. For rural people, livestock shows, festivals, and markets offer a break from a life of hard work in isolated communities. Urban Argentines head to the lakes in the southern Andes and the hills of Cordóba to camp, fish, and have outdoor asados. The wealthy travel to country houses, which may have swimming pools and tennis courts. Many such houses are just 45 minutes from Buenos Aires and stand together inside guarded walls.

Many students celebrate the end of secondary school with a *viaje de egresados*, or graduation trip. They often spend around 10 days in the Patagonian ski resort of Bariloche. During the day, some teens hit the slopes, skiing recklessly, often for the first time. Others

viaje de egresados
(bee-AH-hay they ey-grey-SAH-thos)

Argentina is famous for the quality of its snow and its ski resorts.

spend their days inside drinking hot chocolate and preparing for all-night dance parties.

Passion for Soccer

Argentine teens are passionate about competitive sports. Tennis is a popular sport with both boys and girls. Most towns have at least one tennis court where young people can practice. Upper-income families visit exclusive sporting clubs to play tennis and sail yachts. Argentine tennis star Gabriela Sabatini inspires many. She began winning international tournaments as a teenager. Girls often are involved in sports such as gymnastics, field hockey, and volleyball. Even roller-skating is a competitive sport in Argentina.

Soccer, called *fútbol*, remains almost exclusively a male sport. A boy's favorite possession is often his soccer ball. Boys who cannot afford one will

fútbol
(FOOT-bohl)

The La Bombonera stadium is home to the Boca Juniors soccer team. The stadium vibrates when fans jump in rhythm.

construct a ball out of socks packed with crumpled, tightly wrapped newspaper. Saturday afternoons find neighborhood children playing informal games in soccer fields, in the street, or in any open space. For low-income children, soccer legends such as Diego Maradona make the sport seem like a possible escape from a difficult life. Maradona grew up in Villa Fiorito, a slum outside of Buenos Aires. He was an exceptional player even as a teenager. He went on to play for teams in Spain and Italy. He also led Argentina's national team to win the 1986 World Cup.

A Dangerous Game

As many as 65,000 fans gather to watch a soccer game in massive stadiums such as the Estadio Monumental Antonio Vespucio Liberti in Buenos Aires. The scene is loud and chaotic. Fans paint their faces with their favorite team's colors. They sing as loudly as possible. They toss streamers from the stands and set off firecrackers, flares, and smoke bombs. Police sometimes have to use tear gas and plastic bullets to keep order. Women and young children rarely go to games, since stadiums can be dangerous places.

Hundreds of gang members known as *barras bravas* often attend. Traditionally their role was to heckle the opposing team. However, today they are armed with knives and guns. They rob people and sell drugs. They even intimidate the players and their managers. Because they are so well organized, police find them hard to control. A former referee said:

Here in South America, in countries where five years ago you'd never be able to imagine that so much soccer-related violence could exist ... organization among barras bravas has reached very highly developed levels ... Groups abroad are copying the chants, the songs, and even the flags that got their start here in Argentina.

barras bravas
(BAH-rrahs BRHA-bahs)

77

Equestrian Games

The Spanish brought horses to Argentina in the 1500s. Some horses escaped and bred in the wild. Today they are prized for their strong bones, the result of limestone-rich soil and vast areas to run. Since there are few organized activities in the countryside, many children learn to ride horses and practice throwing lassos at an early age. They participate in rodeos called *domas*. There they can show off their skills before crowds egging the horses on by cheering *"¡Arre! ¡Arre!"*

Argentines love to play games on horseback. Some games played today were developed by indigenous people and later by gauchos. In the original game of *pato*, the players placed a bird in a basket. A rider attempted to carry the bird home as other riders tried to stop him any way they could, even

domas
(DO-mahs)

arre
(aH-rehh)

pato
(PAH-toh)

The word doma comes from the Spanish verb that means "to domesticate an animal."

Argentina is home to some of the best polo players in the world.

by slashing off his saddle. People now play the game with a leather ball with handles. Players throw the ball among themselves and score goals by tossing it into a hoop. In another traditional game called *sortija*, a galloping rider tries to run a thin stick through a ring, sometimes as small as a wed-

sortija
(sohr-TEE-hah)

ding ring, hanging from a pole.

The English introduced polo more than a century ago. Riders use mallets to move a wooden ball across a field into a goal. Because horses are inexpensive in Argentina, polo is more affordable than in other parts of the world. Like soccer, polo offers the promise of escape to a luxurious life. Ranch workers with access to horses and practice fields may dream of fame and fortune as a polo player. The best players often have grown up on their families' large farms, playing on teams with fathers, sons, uncles, and cousins. While most players are men, women and young people can compete in separate tournaments. Children also play informally on their family horses or on bicycles.

The Little and Big Screens

Argentines enjoy a lively social life even when watching television. The most animated gatherings for any Argentine happen during televised soccer matches on Friday and Saturday evenings and Sunday afternoons. In cafés and restaurants, soccer games blare from television sets. Customers cheer wildly and set off fireworks on the sidewalk to celebrate their team's goals. Fans crowd the streets after games, banging drums and honking their horns endlessly. When Argentina won the World Cup in 1978 and 1986, soccer fanatics poured out to celebrate, dancing on bus roofs in traffic-jammed streets.

Argentines, like other Latin Americans, long have enjoyed watching *telenovelas,* or soap operas. These shows have a set number of episodes. Recent shows have been targeted at teens and revolve around young characters. The programs are so popular that teens order CDs of the

telenovelas
(teh-leh-noh-VEH-las)

Soccer fans cheered an Argentina during the 2006 World Cup.

show's music. They also buy clothing, cosmetics, and other products related to the show. Teens can even receive instant messages about the show on their cell phones.

Teens also enjoy watching music

videos and playing video games together. They like renting videos or going out to movie theaters. American movies dubbed into Spanish are favorites. However, Argentine films also have enjoyed international success. Several movies have probed the difficult subject of the recent military dictatorship. For example, *The Official Story* is about a woman who discovers that the biological mother of her adopted child was kidnapped during the Dirty War.

Looking Ahead

TODAY A WEALTH OF RESOURCES OFFERS ARGENTINA'S TEENS BOTH OPPORTUNITIES AND CHALLENGES. Immigrants from around the world have shaped their country's cultural traditions. Yet recent immigration from nearby countries has created fierce job competition for low-income Argentine families. City life offers many activities, from tango halls to all-night bookstores to famous universities. Yet residents from the countryside flood the cities hoping for better jobs, only to end up in slums where their lives are often miserable. Cattle, food crops, and energy reserves provide Argentina the raw materials it needs to create wealth for the benefit of all its citizens. Yet the economy's instability periodically has disrupted the daily lives of its people.

Argentina's teens are poised to take on these challenges. The country's high literacy rate and emphasis on education have produced a young population ready to enter the work force. Teens also have the advantage of supportive families who continue to help them well into adulthood. They are inclined to help others and increasingly are volunteering to assist the disadvantaged. Today's teens must work hard to fulfill Argentina's potential to be prosperous and stable, and to be culturally diverse and unified.

At a Glance

Official name: República Argentina

Capital: Buenos Aires

People

Population: 40,482,000

Population by age group:
0-14 years: 24.9%
15-64 years: 64.4%
65 years and over: 10.7%

Life expectancy at birth: 76.32 years

Official language: Spanish

Other common languages: English, Italian, German, French

Religion:
Roman Catholic: 92%
Protestant: 2%
Jewish: 2%
Other: 4%

Legal ages:
Alcohol consumption: 18
Driver's license: 18
Employment: 14 (except for children working in farming and family-run businesses)
Leave school: 14
Marriage: 21
Military service: 18
Voting: 18

Government

Type of government: Republic

Chief of state and head of government: President and vice president, elected by popular vote

Lawmaking body: Bicameral National Congress, consisting of Senate and Chamber of Deputies

Administrative divisions: 23 provinces and one federal district

Independence: July 9, 1816 (from Spain)

National symbol: Three equal horizontal bands of light blue (top), white, and light blue; centered in the white band is a radiant yellow sun with a human face known as the Sun of May, representing Argentina's freedom from Spain

Geography

Total area: 1,068,296 square miles (2,766,890 square km)

Climate: Mostly temperate; arid in southeast; subantarctic in southwest

Highest point: Cerro Aconcagua, 22,834 feet (6,960 meters)

Lowest point: Laguna del Carbon, 344 feet (105 meters) below sea level

Major rivers and lakes: Paraná, Paraguay, Rio de la Plata, Uruguay

Major landforms: Paraná Plateau, Gran Chaco, Pampas, Monte, plateau known as Patagonia, Andes mountains

Economy

Currency: Argentine peso

Population below poverty line: 23%

Major natural resources: Lead, zinc, tin, copper, salt, oil, coal, sunflower seeds, lemons, soybeans, grapes, corn, tobacco, peanuts, tea, wheat, livestock

Major agricultural products: Sunflower seeds, lemons, soybeans, grapes, corn, tobacco, peanuts, tea, wheat, livestock

Major exports: Soybeans and derivatives, petroleum and gas, vehicles, corn, wheat

Major imports: Machinery, petroleum and natural gas, motor vehicles, organic chemicals, plastics

Historical Timeline

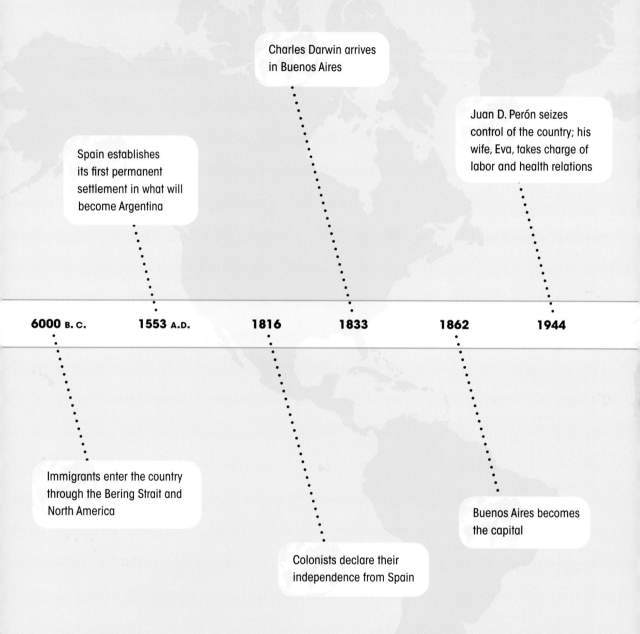

Charles Darwin arrives in Buenos Aires

Juan D. Perón seizes control of the country; his wife, Eva, takes charge of labor and health relations

Spain establishes its first permanent settlement in what will become Argentina

6000 B. C.   **1553** A.D.   **1816**   **1833**   **1862**   **1944**

Immigrants enter the country through the Bering Strait and North America

Buenos Aires becomes the capital

Colonists declare their independence from Spain

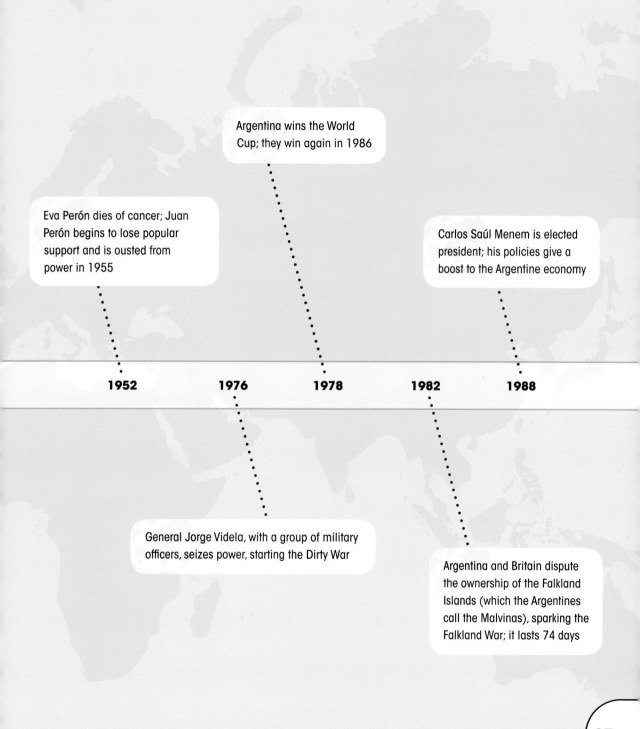

Argentina wins the World
Cup; they win again in 1986

Eva Perón dies of cancer; Juan
Perón begins to lose popular
support and is ousted from
power in 1955

Carlos Saúl Menem is elected
president; his policies give a
boost to the Argentine economy

1952   **1976**   **1978**   **1982**   **1988**

General Jorge Videla, with a group of military
officers, seizes power, starting the Dirty War

Argentina and Britain dispute
the ownership of the Falkland
Islands (which the Argentines
call the Malvinas), sparking the
Falkland War; it lasts 74 days

Historical Timeline

The economy collapses, leading to protests and rioting; the country goes through five presidents in 10 days; thousands of people are thrown into poverty

Cristina Fernández de Kirchner becomes president, making her Argentina's first directly elected female president; Argentines protest in Buenos Aires to raise awareness of hunger and poverty; Argentina and Brazil embark on their first joint space mission with a successful rocket launch into space

1994   **2001**   **2004**   **2007**   **2008**

A terrorist attack at a Buenos Aires Jewish community center kills 85 people and causes about 300 injuries; no one is convicted in the attack

After a nightclub fire kills more than 200 people, thousands protest the government's failure to enforce safety codes

Argentina defeats Nigeria in soccer at the Beijing Olympics; this is the team's second consecutive gold medal win

Glossary

crisis	time of great trouble
economy	way a country produces, distributes, and uses its money, goods, natural resources, and services
indigenous	native to a place
illiterate	inability to read or write
infant mortality	death rate during the first year of life
inflation	amount that prices rise during a certain time period
installments	parts of a debt to be paid at regular intervals over a certain period of time
isolated	separate, solitary
migrant	people who move to new areas or countries, often in search of work
resource	something that lies ready for use
suburb	mostly residential communities that are immediately outside of city limits
tuition	fee paid to attend a school

Additional Resources

FURTHER READING

Fiction and nonfiction titles to enhance your introduction to teens in Argentina, past and present.

Fraggalosch, Audrey, Michael Denman, and William Huiett. *Land of the Wild Llama: A Story of the Patagonian Andes*. Norwalk, Conn.: Soundprints, 2002.

Shields, Charles J. *Discovering South America: Argentina*. Philadelphia: Mason Crest Publishers, 2004.

Stille, Darlene. *Eva Peron: First Lady of Argentina*. Minneapolis: Compass Point Books, 2006.

Kalnay, Francis. *Chucaro: Wild Pony of the Pampa*. New York: Walker and Co, 1993.

Van Laan, Nancy. *The Magic Bean Tree: A Legend from Argentina*. Boston: Houghton Mifflin Co., 1998.

ON THE WEB

For more information on this topic, use FactHound.

1. Go to www.facthound.com
2. Choose your grade level.
3. Begin your search.

This book's ID number is 9780756540371
FactHound will find the best sites for you.

Look for more Global Connections books.

Source Notes

Page 16, sidebar, line 9: Marcos Morales. E-mail interview.

Page 23, sidebar, column 2, line 3: Ibid.

Page 27, sidebar, line 27: Helen Popper. "Argentine Drug Law Plan Sparks Debate in Slums." 18 Aug. 2008. 20 Aug. 2008. www.reuters.com/article/worldNews/idUSN183957 0120080818?feedType=RSS&feedName=worldNews

Page 29, column 1, line 35: Alejandra Labanca. "Nobody's Children." *The Miami Herald*. 27 Nov. 2006. 19 July 2008. www.miamiherald.com/multimedia/news/ americas/argentina/index.html

Page 33, column 2, line 8: Daniel Schweimler. "Argentine Indigneous in Protest." *BBC News*. 6 Nov. 2006. 15 Aug. 2008. http://news.bbc.co.uk/2/hi/americas/7082190.stm

Page 46, sidebar, column 2, line 6: Alexi Barrionuevo. "In Macho Argentina, a New Beacon For Gay Tourists." *The New York Times*. 3 Dec. 2007. 1 Aug. 2008. www.nytimes.com/2007/12/03/world/americas/03argentina. html?_r=1&fta=y&oref=slogin

Page 56, sidebar, column 2, line 3: Thomas C. Wright. *State Terrorism in Latin America*. Lanham, Md.: Rowman & Littlefield, 2007. http://books.google.com/ books?id=ztjV7GVNeiAC

Page 67, column 1, line 8: Sara Miller Llana. "Argentina Gets Set to Elect its 'Hillary'." *The Christian Science Monitor*. 26 Oc. 2007. 5 Aug. 2008. www.csmonitor.com/2007/1026/p01s06-woam.html?page=1

Page 77, sidebar, column 2, line 10: Monte Reel. "Argentina's Soccer Gangs Test Limits of Public Tolerance." *The Washington Post*. 24 Feb. 2007. 16 Aug. 2008. www.washingtonpost.com/wp-dyn/content/ article/2007/02/23/AR2007022301677.html

Pages 84–85, At A Glance: Argentina. Central Intelligence Agency. *The World Factbook—Argentina*. 4 Sept. 2008. 25 Sept. 2008. https://www.cia.gov/library/publications/the-world-factbook/ geos/ar.html

Barrionuevo, Alexei. "Cheap Cocaine Floods Argentina, Devouring Lives." *The New York Times*. 23 Feb. 2008. 8 July 2008. www.nytimes.com/2008/02/23/world/americas/23argentina.html?scp=3&sq=argentina+children&st=nyt

Cagliani, Martín. "Solar Energy for 85 Rural Schools in Argentina." *Green Options Media*. 12 March 2008. 30 April 2008. http://ecoworldly.com/2008/03/12/solar-energy-for-85-rural-schools-in-argentina/

Grady, Denise. "In Argentina, a Museum Unveils a Long-Frozen Maiden." *The New York Times*. 11 Sept. 2007. 30 April 2008. www.nytimes.com/2007/09/11/science/11mummu.html?scp=1&sq=argentina+children&st=nyt

Labanca, Alejandra. "Nobody's Children." *The Miami Herald*. 27 Nov. 2006. 30 April 20008. www.miamiherald.com/multimedia/news/americas/argentina/index.html

Labanca, Alejandra. "Teens crave glue, 'paco'—'You have to do drugs to belong'." *The Miami Herald*. 27 Nov. 2006. 30 April 2008. www.miamiherald.com/multimedia/news/americas/argentina/side1.html

Labanca, Alejandra. "The Street Children of Buenos Aires." *The Miami Herald*. 27 Nov. 2006. 30 April 2008. www.miamiherald.com/multimedia/news/americas/argentina/side2.html

Lonely Planet. "Argentina." 2008. 26 Aug. 2008. www.lonelyplanet.com/worldguide/argentina/

Pearce, Nick. "Cry for Us, Argentina." *Progress*. 17 Jan. 2007. 30 April 2008. www.progressonline.org.uk/Magazine/article.asp?a=1540

Reel, Monte. "In Rural Argentina, the Legacy of Migration." *The Washington Post*. 14 Sept. 2007. 30 April 2008. www.washingtonpost.com/wp-dyn/content/article/2007/09/13/AR2007091302424.html

Reel, Monte. "Latin Telenovelas Aim for Teens." *St. Augustine Record*. 19 Feb. 2008. 30 April 2008. www.staugustine.com/stories/041705/wor_3019801.shtml

Rohter, Larry. "A Widening Gap Erodes Argentina's Egalitarian Image." *The New York Times*. 25 Dec. 2006. 30 April 2008. www.nytimes.com/2006/12/25/world/americas/25argentina.html?scp=14&sq=argentina+children&st=nyt

Rosenberg, Fernando. "Grupo de Arte Callejero (Street Art Group)." *E-misférica Journal*. 26 Oct. 2006. 30 April 2008. www.hemisphericinstitute.org/journal/april percent202006/sentations/3*percent20Grupo percent20depercent20Artepercent20Callejero/abstract.html

Schweimler, Daniel. "Argentine Indigenous in Protest." *BBC News*. 6 Nov. 2007. 30 April 2008. http:/news.bbc.co.uk/2/hi/americas/7082190.stm

Sica, Gregory. "Olympic Soccer Argentina-Brazil: Argentina and Brazil Clash in Olympic Games Semifinal." *International Soccer*. 18 Aug. 2008. 27 Aug. 2008. http://internationalsoccer.suite101.com/article.cfm/olympic_soccer_argentinabrazil

Index

About the Author
Danielle Smith-Llera

Danielle Smith-Llera has taught literature, writing, history, and visual arts to students ranging from elementary school to college. She is also a widely exhibited visual artist and plays violin in chamber groups. Danielle earned an undergraduate degree in English and visual arts from Harvard University and an M.F.A. from Old Dominion University. She lives with her family on the marshy edge of the Chesapeake Bay in Norfolk, Virginia.

About the Content Adviser
David William Foster

David William Foster is Regents' Professor of Spanish and Women and Gender Studies at Arizona State University. He specializes in Latin American urban culture, with emphasis on gender identities and Jewish Diaspora culture. He has held Fulbright appointments in Argentina, Brazil, and Uruguay, and has also taught in Chile.